P9-DWG-280

The Loneliness Machine

CALGARY PUBLIC LIBRARY

JAN ⁻ 2014

The Loneliness Machine

Aaron Giovannone

INSOMNIAC PRESS

Copyright © 2013 by Aaron Giovannone

Edited for the press by Sachiko Murakami

All rights reserved. No part of this publication may be
reproduced, stored in a retrieval system or transmitted, in any form or by any
means, without the prior written permission of the publisher or, in the case of
photocopying or other reprographic copying, a licence from
Access Copyright, 1 Yonge Street, Suite 1900, Toronto, ON M5E 1E5

Library and Archives Canada Cataloguing in Publication

Giovannone, Aaron, 1979-, author
The loneliness machine / Aaron Giovannone.

Poems.
ISBN 978-1-55483-107-4 (pbk.)

I. Title.

PS8613.I68L65 2013   C811'.6   C2013-906509-1

The publisher gratefully acknowledges the support of the Canada Council, the
Ontario Arts Council, and the Department of Canadian Heritage through
the Canada Book Fund.

Printed and bound in Canada

Insomniac Press
520 Princess Avenue, London, Ontario, Canada, N6B 2B8
www.insomniacpress.com

ONTARIO ARTS COUNCIL
CONSEIL DES ARTS DE L'ONTARIO

For Mary Margaret "My Mom" Griffiths

Contents

I.

II.

III.

I.

Burnt Offering

You said *go to bed.*
I'm in bed.

This is my place.
This is me.

It's hard for me to be in the mood
you need me to be in right now.

You say *panzerotti,*
but I think *Hot Pocket.*

I am trying to get at something,
and I want to talk plainly to you.

A single,
slow clapping.

Thank you.

Stockholm Syndrome

Hi, everyone. It's Aaron.
How are you? Okay great.

Is a representative
from the Canada Council here?

A special welcome to you
and to all the ladies celebrating a birthday.

We're on vacation in here.
There's lots of light in the margins.

You feel the rhythm of your attention
to your pockets, your phone, your fingertips.

Hey, did you hear that Iran
is designing its own internet?

This poem is *our* own internet,
and one of the rules of our internet is:

You must take a shot of Wild Turkey
when you read the word *poem* in this poem.

Check your phone.
Who's that messaging you?

Surprise!
It's me!

And what does the message say?
Poem, poem, poem!

Just Be Cool

I'm sitting at a picnic table
at the beach.
No use pretending I'm not.

You?

You're reading this poem
in my prize-winning collection,
The Loneliness Machine.

Me?

I live on the ground floor,
so there's no point
in jumping out of the window.

You?

Hearing me read,
you think you've finally found
a shoe that breathes.

Me?
Who's asking?
You?

O heavens!
O non-existing heavens!
Why am I yelling?

Pop the Trunk

It's unseasonably warm,
every season.
Global warming
pools around our ankles.

Instead of Grandpa,
we have an arrangement
of thank-you cards
from transplantees.

METAPHOR ALERT!
A cruise ship sinks off the coast of Tuscany,
flickering its lights,
raising sea levels all over the globe.

I am part of the problem
because I love my new cell phone.
If you send me a text message,
my face will light up.

Please.
My number is
403-829-1369
That's my real number.

Seriously.
I'm up late.
That number again:
403-829-1369.

The Thin Scholar

The neoliberal politics
of shrimp poppers
with jalapeno salsa.

I come to you with joy,
knowing joy is a surplus value
extracted from a sad person.

I want to win an award,
invite everyone to the gala,
except you, Dad.

A severed head found in a park.
Not my head.
Not anyone I know.

I arrive at a profound ambivalence.
I both *am* and *am not*,
the *not* being the condition of the *am*.

You aren't me,
but I'd like you to be.
I am coming to cut your head off.

Shrimp poppers, anybody?
A man,
let's call him

"Aaron,"
squirms in his chair
because he's at a creative impasse.

Time to Take Me Seriously

You are already broken.
I am already broken.
It doesn't matter
what pronoun one uses.

Everybody is broken.
Except joggers.
They've temporarily forgotten
about being broken.

A man lurches down the sidewalk,
yelling like crazy.
He wears a yellow hard hat
because he's working

to make us feel less broken
by comparison.
I snip the long stems
of red carnations.

I love paper books
more because they're dying.
I love the dying more
because it's less commitment.

With soft watery eyes,
I look at a wiener dog
with soft watery eyes.
I'm on the leash now.

A Famous Quotation Is Hidden in This Poem

This is a poem
if you believe.
I stare into my phone

when there's nothing to do
but face the emptiness.
I touch the screen.

No new messages.
I don't want to live
with no new messages.

I'm afraid of life,
so I'm scripting it.
I'll prove it to you.

Read this line,
now this one.
Ha!

The lyf so short,
the craft
so longe to lerne.

Did you get it?
That's Chaucer.
Ha!

My Kingdom for a Belmont King Size

What's your plan tonight, guys?
Loneliness?
Poetry and loneliness?
Can I bum a cigarette?

A single cigarette
I'll carry in my heart,
which has a silhouette
of a cigarette cut out of it.

I brush my teeth,
my subjectivity breaking apart.
A rhythm I follow,
a structure so ineluctable.

Guys, I'm not strong enough
to escape my point of view.
I'd cross to the other sidewalk
to avoid you.

Cranberry Juice

You think *detoxification*.
I think *retoxification*.
The sun ages me.

Also, vodka
and chocolate
chocolate chip ice cream.

I've got silver fillings.
The dentist drilled the rot,
replaced it with the blood of robots.

Like a solar panel,
I gather li'l bits of energy
from smiles as I go.

How did I become a collage
of quips, quotes, anecdotes,
and rhetorical questions?

I sip juice from concentrate.
My teeth aren't human.
They pulsate.

Lake Poet

I am at a lake.
I am a Lake Poet now.
Giant poodles strut
like miniature bears on leashes.

They're not bears,
obviously.
A moment is binary.
It asks *yes* or *no*.

I am a slow computer,
growing slower.
Kids toss a frisbee.
They're terrible at frisbee.

They've thrown the frisbee into a tree.
They chuck rocks at the tree
to knock the frisbee down.
I am a Lake Poet now.

Going *Commando*
after David McGimpsey

I've dipped my nose
in an ice cream cone.
I look towards the empty horizon.

I smell the helicopter coming.
Arnold Schwarzenegger thumps me in the stomach
then stuffs my body in a garden shed.

Who am I?
I am Colombian Henchman Number Five.
I wish Arnold were my dad.

The stunt guys show me how to get shot:
I fling my arms out like this,
my soul jangling like Alyssa Milano's bracelets.

If I feel physically
like the top of my head were taken off....
No, Emily Dickinson, it's not *poetry,*

it's a circular saw blade
that Arnold frisbeed at me,
which physically chopped the top of my head off.

Entertain Me

A woman on TV in Orange County
snaps her phone shut.
I want her to call me.

People with flat bellies
don't eat spoonfuls of peanut butter
at 1:48 a.m.

I was more optimistic at 1:44 a.m.
At around 1:45 a.m.,
things took a turn for the worse.

In a heartfelt conversation,
Becky Conner explains her elopement
to her dad, John Goodman.

She says she was
just another mouth to feed.
She doesn't say *elopement,*

that's my word.
It's been a long time since I've had
a heartfelt conversation.

Once I dreamed I ate Domino's
in the opening sequence
with the Conner family.

When I woke up on the couch
with a pizza box on my chest,
Roseanne was on TV.

Dear Facebook Friend

Sometimes I sit looking at Facebook,
like *really* leaning into my computer
as if I were leaning out of a window
into the sunshine.

Dear Facebook Friend,
remember when we sat on a bench together
with ice cream cones,
the melt running down our fingers?

We smiled at each other,
thinking about being naked.
Well, I don't know what you were thinking about.

The bench's wire mesh
pressed into the flesh of our bums,
and the sun cut our shapes out on the pavement
like paper dolls.

Dear Facebook Friend,
I like your status update.

In my memories, there are always
lots of people,
and you are one of them.

I Was Surrounded by Things Existing Nonchalantly

You have to be careful
because you could smell bad
and you wouldn't know.

The darkness paints and repaints
the windowpane the exact colour
of what's happening inside.

What's happening outside?
How much night separates/
connects two fields of pumpkins?

A story about dogs
sniffs through the tall grass
and wanders into the woods.

Like Hamlet, it comes back
resolved "to do something"
but not sure what.

I Don't Know Anyone in the Room

I know everyone in the room.
They bleed from the peripheries of my poppy,
which is too high on my lapel and threatens my eye.

Who yells *yeah, yeah* anymore,
and how could I feel its dismissal so deeply?
Like the heel you swivelled on when our eyes met,

I have been scrubbed by happenings for years.
I'm used to memory loss as conversation starter, like
how do you tie a scarf with style? and

my great-great-uncle was hit by a train in 1909.
I'm sorry to hear that said the archivist.
Yeah, yeah.

Funny Cat Video

A letter slid under your door.
You unfold it.

It reads *No, don't get up.*
It's sprinkled with words like:

sprinkled, words, like.
The phrase *English Literature*

is hyperlinked in this note.
I'm glad you laughed at that.

It's the Power Outage Edition
of our relationship.

What are you thinking?
I don't need to know.

But are you thinking of me a little?
Come on.

My body's percentage of water
changes as I drink a glass of water.

Let's Make Our Lives Amazing

You close your eyes
when the sun's too bright,
privatizing it inside you.

You photosynthesize, sort of.
You convert light into being.
This is a good business model.

The suburbs swirl into a giant cochlea,
listening to our jet take off.
But who are "we"?

The page tilts in the light
like the airplane's wings.
Let me help you, like poetry helped me.

What Am I Supposed to Do?

I pull on a woolly blue sweater,
one with the neck too tight,
and surface, out of breath.

Turning a corner, a minivan's headlights
spill across the frosty asphalt
like a bucket of diamonds.

I'm not blaming anyone,
but the cold snap has frozen
the songbirds' feathers

and turned them into snowflakes.
Yes, I'm trying to build irony into this,
but what you read has passed

under the eyes of editors who laugh,
who stuff rejection notes in envelopes,
run their tongues along bitter glue, and smile.

When will they realize
that I have feelings too
and that I'm all tangled up

in a string of Christmas lights?
Cold air whips too easily
through sweatpants.

The extension cord crackles,
tingling my fingers,
then darkness snaps on.

What Does It All Mean?

Every moment I'm away from my computer
is a moment I can write about at my computer,
because every moment is precious.

If you don't enjoy reading this,
imagine how I feel thinking it.
A cough from the audience at the quiet part

while my cell phone buzzes on my desk.
It's my friend Jason texting to say
just finish the poem. Okay.

Goodnight, Moon,
goodnight, Stars.
I am comfortable in my corner of the universe.

The quote, unquote real world
isn't funny, it's horrible.
There's capitalism out there.

That's why I'm moving home with Mom.
She picks me up at the airport
in the rusting Chevy Venture

that I like to call the *Chevy Monster*.
We hug. I load my luggage
beside her mobility scooter.

Driving home, I choose
a station that plays "Fergalicious."
Mom reaches for the dial.

Can I Go Now?

I need to finish this.

My show is starting in a half hour.
(*Extras*, starring Ricky Gervais.)

Yes, these are old notes,
and the darkness is touching me.

Twenty minutes now,
and what I've breathed out

I breathe in again,
like the sigh of the metro's slipstream.

I went downstairs for a glass of water
and lost a few more minutes.

Back then, they were building
the Bibliothèque nationale.

The machines shook my bed most mornings,
but I'm actually asleep right now.

Two minutes left.

II.

Pennian Interlude

Nuotatore

Dormiva...?
    Poi si tolse e si stirò.
Guardò con occhi lenti l'acqua. Un guizzo
il suo corpo.
    Così lasciò la terra.

Swimmer

Was he sleeping...?
    He stood and stretched.
With slow eyes, he watched the water. A flicker,
his body.
    This is how he left the earth.

    —Sandro Penna (1906–1977)

If I'm walking alone down the gravel path
beside the old canal
that rushes and trips over itself,

there's probably a boy in the neighbourhood
lying on his parents' lawn
with his eyes wide open.

Everybody's alone, I know that.
But some nights we look at the same stars
and feel the same feelings.

(And I know Sandro Penna wrote a poem kind of like
    this.)

The dawn makes a lot of noise,
but it's the noise of "things," not people.

Sometimes it's the neighbour whistling to his dog,
but it's not really him.
It's only a thin voice calling the daylight out.

At the bottom of our hill,
it's the whoosh of cars,
and further down the valley,
it's the old canal falling over its broken locks.

Then it's all drowned out
by Mom roaring away on the lawn mower....

The park listened to secrets
murmured by the sun.

I was jogging.
Over my footfalls
I couldn't hear them.

I don't want poetry
of delicate words
(the cold sun in March
on shivering plantain
leaves, a green too clear).

In my neighbourhood,
there aren't plantain trees.

Like a high-school all-star
throwing a javelin,
my poetry
will hurl itself into "The Infinite."
Do you know that poem by Leopardi?

On the opposite bank of the canal,
their laughter slashes through the willows.

The girl hushes the loudest boy,
who hadn't seen me.

Now it's just my feet on the gravel.

The young man reading
listens to the neighbours'
kids swimming in their pool.

Not understanding anything,
he looks at the afternoon sun
on his arm and blank notebook.

The sun wouldn't die in the café
where a young man sat reading.

He hunched over, ignoring the others
because they weren't there to see him.

The sun connected and divided us.
Both of us were dying and didn't know it.

It was the café
where the doors
continually whoosh open.

Because of that he thought
she was coming back.
But she wasn't.

You're far away.

Colours surround you,
but I can't see them.

Colours surround me,
but I can't see them.

Why did we come down to the canal so late?
The canal stumbles down to the lake
and reaches out to the city,
where I don't know anyone.

You will be friends with the most disparate of people,
and then you won't be friends anymore.
This is what I'd say to your nineteen-year-old eyes,
shining like street lamps in the water.

The bench waits for me
even when I'm sitting on it.

The broken lock washes over
with forgetfulness.

I wonder if I can start over.

A night in early summer.
The window brims
with a family's image.
My silence on the sidewalk.

Strobe lights, don't tell me
that the night isn't beautiful.

Look at the kids dancing,
moving like ancient

friezes.
You stop-motion their happiness.

Strobe lights,
counting out the evenings
with snapping fingers,

don't tell me the night isn't beautiful.

Do you think the springtime knows
this sweetness is mine and has nothing to do with it?

Like the teen sleeping wrapped up in himself,
not looking for anything.

I think slowly in the spring morning.
I feel—*sento*—
I smell the lilacs opening.

How long do lilacs last?

Big dreaming tree,
are you telling me
your heart doesn't beat harder

when the sun surprises you
with a gecko's small heartbeat
between your fingers?

My heart pounds harder,
and I'm not doing anything.
I'm just leaning against you.

Our house missed the sunset
when it got careless
and fell asleep.

Beside my mother watching TV,
we're quiet, faced with a secret
so precious we keep it forever.

The old canal kept me happy,
happier than my street, which was empty,

except for my feet running on the sidewalk
and my heavy breathing.

But what I loved most about you, O suburb,
was sleeping, breathing quietly.

Behind every curtain,
it would never wake up.

Goodbye to you,
who enters the darkness.

My path's along the canal,
until the world returns.

From time to time, a secret lights up
the cell phone in my pocket.

But when he was finally lost, and the water
darkened where he had sunk,
on the bank beside me I saw Sandro Penna.

How many times had his baby blue *Poesie*
darkened in my hand,
going into my knapsack?

III.

Come In

A knock.
A light rapping.
Repeated.
Silence.
The tinkle of keys.
The deadbolt turns.
The door swings open and rattles against the wall.
You come in and hang up the keys.
You saunter in, singing to yourself.
You yell *hello*.
You come in, hauling a plastic grocery bag stretched full.
You wipe your boots on the mat.
You come in, chatting with someone who's still outside.
    (This person will never come in.)
You come in.
Quietly.
I never get beyond this point.
You kick the door off the hinges
because your arms are full of roses.
You come in laughing,
and someone following you in is laughing.

The Trees Bend Towards a Vanishing Point

for Thom & Tyler

i.

The trees bend towards a vanishing point
in the sky. You swing
the embers from a burning stick,
beating fireflies into luminescence.

In two days, you will have forgotten your other life.

ii.

Funny how one inch this way
is no longer too much fire.

The embers pixelate, humming.
Like a splash of liquid citronella,
you're woken up by a crash

in the greendark gone quiet
under your flashlight's interrogation.

iii.

The hari-kari of another water bottle
you crush against your sternum for recycling.

While we lie quietly in the tent,
the lightning snaps photos
of our abandoned campsite.

The storm tings and pings on the tent.
You stare off into your book.

iv.

The monster waiting in the sand-
hole gulps bucketfuls of water.

The kids pad off screaming
for more with rattling buckets.

v.

After beating through the sand-coloured waves,
you couldn't touch bottom.

With eyes clenched, your stomach
bottomed out in shock.

Then toes surprised by pebbles
rolling under you, the waves over you.

A Poem Isn't a Memory
for A.S.

A poem isn't a memory.
When I read it again,
I remember that isn't what happened.

A poem is a way of being alone.
But I'd rather
have my hand on your thigh.

My hand's on my thigh.
I sink into this leather chair
and sink into a drink
with comfortable friends.

Stella sewed "Cuddlebots"
from old sweatshirts
that belonged to her baby's grandfather.
Thus the old man lives
in every squeeze of her baby's fingers.

I wish I knew a girl in this city
who I could text
instead of scribbling notes for a poem.

This Cuddlebot has button eyes
and looks into mine,
downloading incredible softness.

I won't get off the couch today.

Of my two thousand daily recommended calories,
more than two thousand
will come from Nutella.

I want to close my eyes
and open them and see you there again.

The Mystery Birds

The mystery birds
sang again all night
outside my window.

I'm trying to leave a crack
in the window at night
so mysteries can come in.

But I also need my sleep.
I'm looking in the mirror.
I look terrible.

In the quiet kitchen,
the sound of gulls
rose from the just-filled

Brita pitcher dripping.
I'm sorry if this is boring
and too intimate

like a pile of wet socks and boxer briefs
that a stranger's removed
from the washing machine for you.

The Loneliness Machine

i.

My thoughts turn towards her
in her room in Pasadena
when I read the word *Pasadena* in a novel.

In a photo booth, we took a photo
with her phone because
the photo booth was broken.

These words are my absence,
unless I'm reading this to you.
In that case, listen, I'm right here.

ii.

I sat in a lecture hall, half-
thinking of you asleep on a plane,
letting that distance settle into my headache.

I listened to myself
answer questions badly
because I was listening to myself.

It was like you (who's gone now)
had laid your head on my chest (which you hadn't),
and I could imagine what you'd heard.

iii.

The same old loneliness
is flapping on the peripheries
like a bird in a palm tree.

On Wikipedia, I'm
looking up the names
of exotic birds. *Guácharo.*

It's a guácharo plucking
my feelings from the air
like mosquitoes.

iv.

Soon we'll pull
the drapes closed.
It's not quite five.

I know a woman
whom I hit on at a conference
is married because

she wrote about it
in an essay.
I just read the essay.

v.

Curtains printed with
twigs, berries, butterflies
flutter, then still, when I close them.

I've closed myself in.
You're sitting next to me.
Boy, you hate this poem.

I just want to be honest.
I want money. I want
money for this.

Hey Up Here

In poems,
there are never iPhones
or fears of venereal disease.

I'm supposed to show intense emotion now.
The glow on the mountainside,
the sun on the glinting condos.

The river that moves so river-like
and doesn't disappoint.
Up here, there's a gravel path

good for Labradors and Pomeranians
and other dog breeds I can't name
because I am a cat person.

You can bring your baby up here
in a stroller and jog behind it
if you're trying to get back in shape.

But hey, you already look great.
I wouldn't worry too much.

Lynn Saw a Ghost
for Bagga

Lynn saw a ghost
in the garden
in a blue dress.

What was the ghost doing? we ask.
Nothing she says.

*And why were you wearing
a blue dress?*
No, the ghost was.

Okay.

Mom knows that ghost.
Once, Grandpa saw it
in a red dress.

What a nice wardrobe says Lynn.

*But why are ghosts
always wearing dresses?* I say.

The day after Grandpa died,
Lynn saw him
in the garden.

What was he doing? we ask.

Looking at the flowers Lynn says.

And what
was he wearing?

The Wrinkle in Things

Snow so thick
I inhale a flake.
With warm socks
everything's better, sadly.

I ask
how long will parsley in the garden last?
Mom says *yes.*
She coughs the word.

I've cut under my lip shaving,
and blood runs down my chin.
Or maybe, like Ozzy,
I've bitten the head off a bat.

A faraway siren.
This doesn't concern me.
I step outside.
The siren's approaching.

Maids of the Mist

for Felicia and Mara

Under Niagara Falls,
it's hard to remember
with the mist beating our faces.

We've knotted the strings
on our rain ponchos' hoods.
Still, they blow off.

I am in the past.
I is the past.
Already!

See how hard my job is?
I forked a barbecued sausage
at the family reunion.

As I mounded my plate,
the chef (some cousin) asked
who are you?

Because I am ignorant,
my voice seems
to come from nowhere.

But really it comes from history,
which is the mist blasting our ponchos
like shower curtains.

Felicia, I'm sorry
your mascara's ruined.
You can't hear me over the roar.

Mara grins nervously.
She's from Italy.
She won't stay long

with us, not here.
Not *here* here.
But not even the falls will,

which erode upriver
one foot each year,
billowing so much mist

that it drips off my rain poncho,
soaking my All Stars,
and squishes with us back to the car.

Hello, St. Catharines

In Tim Hortons, the summer camp photos
behind plexiglass fade in the sun,
just like the real children lose their tans.

A feeling struggles at sunset
when my neighbourhood is dipped in gold
and left in memory a moment.

Around my glowing cell phone,
the dark is always closing in.
It generates a lot of love between us.

We Will Hang Out As Long As We Can Until We Are Sick of Each Other

for Hamish, a baby

It's not for the faint of heart.
I'm not faint of heart.

I am a robot.
The oscillating fan
transforms Chris's voice.

Listen to me, Hamish.
I am your father.
Your father is a robot.

Hamish crawls across the floor.
Supersonic jets blast by.

We run outside.
The jets are nowhere to be seen.

I hope the pilots weren't drunk last night
like I was.

I hope the pilots
are Tom Cruise in aviators in *Top Gun*.

Hamish crawls like a drunken man
onto the plush blue carpet.

Pilots must be better people than us.

Chris throws Hamish
into the air.

Hamish giggles
like a baby.

He might throw up.

Acknowledgements

Thank you, Sachiko Murakami, for editing and for
encouraging "AG."

Thank you, Mike O'Connor and Dan Varrette, for
designing and for copy-editing.

Thank you, Shawn Mankowske, for the cover.

Thank you, Robert Majzels, for reading "Pennian
Interlude." And for all that you do.

Grazie, Sandro Penna.

Thank you, Jason Christie, for your friendship and for
your brilliance.

Thank you, Stella, Oscar (the baby in "A Poem Isn't a
Memory"), Lynn, Mara, Felicia, Chris, and
Hamish, for appearing in these poems. I hope you
don't mind.

Any resemblance to Stella, Oscar, Lynn, Mara, Felicia,
Chris, or Hamish is purely coincidental.

Thank you, Calgary friends and writers, especially
those who frequent Natalie Simpson's Sunday
afternoons at the Kensington Pub: Jani Krulc,
Naomi Lewis, Marc Lynch, Colin Martin, Nikki
Sheppy, Michael Yip, and many others.

Thank you, Okanagan friends and writers Jake
Kennedy and kevin mcpherson eckhoff, for being
the lives of the party.

Thank you, friends, colleagues, and mentors from the
University of Calgary, especially Christian Bök,

Kathleen Brown, Francesca Cadel, Michael Tavel Clarke, Jon Kertzer, Matt Kriz, Harry Vanderlist, and Tom Wayman.

Thank you, friends, colleagues, and mentors from Brock University, especially Jesse Arseneault, Greg Betts, Adam Dickinson, Monica Drenth, and Jesse Hutchison.

Thank you, Palmer Olson and Ryan McClure Scotch, for being Perfect Uncles.

Thank you, Andrea, Jill, and Paul, for the board games, dinners, and dishes.

Grazie, Luciano, Davide, e tutti gli amici castelluciani. Trattate bene uno straniero che ogni tanto torna fra di voi.

Thank you, *Descant*, for publishing "Come In."

Thank you, *Grain*, for publishing "The Trees Bend Towards a Vanishing Point."

Thank you, *Contemporary Verse 2*, for publishing "Hello, St. Catharines."

Thank you, *Prairie Fire*, for publishing "A Poem Isn't a Memory" and "Dear Facebook Friend."

Thank you, *PRISM international*, for publishing "Lynn Saw a Ghost."

Finally:

Grazie, Zia Ada e Zia Bianca. Vi voglio un mondo di bene.

Thank you, Sarah, for teaching yoga and for driving Beamers.

Thank you, pals eternal Thom, Tyler, and Jen.

Thank you, Mom, for everything all of the time.